PITFALLS OF ENTREPRENEURSHIP

Andrea Evans-Dixon

Disclaimer

This book is designed to bring awareness to the various ways those considering entrepreneurship can be sidetracked in pursuit of their dreams. The author does not claim that the pitfalls shared within the book are ones that the reader will experience. The information shared within this book highlights a few difficulties and drawbacks that the author experienced and how she overcame them. Sound efforts have been made for content accuracy. You hereby agree never to sue or hold the author liable for any claims or similarities arising from the information contained within this book. Any likenesses to real persons, alive or deceased, or personal experiences are merely coincidental. You agree to be bound by this disclaimer.

Dedication

This book is dedicated to my husband, J. Fred Dixon Jr., who from the day we met has always encouraged, supported and, most importantly, covered me without ceasing in prayer. You have always had the right words to say that provide the boost I need to keep going and never give up. God saw fit to align our paths to cross twice in our earthly lives and, fortunately for me, I did not miss his blessing the second time. You are truly my angel on earth.

I also dedicate this book to my nephew, Anthony (Double A) and nieces, Alaina and Alaisha, whom I pray will become entrepreneurs. May you dream big and always believe in yourselves. Let no one define who you are, what you can achieve and what you are worth, and never settle for less than your best.

WHAT'S INSIDE

Acknowledgements

Chronicling my experience and lessons learned thus far as an entrepreneur required the assistance and prayers of many. I am truly grateful to everyone who made a contribution to the book. Thank you for everything you have done, big or small, to encourage me in its completion.

To my writing coach and mentor, Michelle Greene-Rhodes, you have been an enormous inspiration to me. Your willingness to see others succeed and the giving spirit you use to elevate others towards fulfilling their calling is exemplary.

To my sister-in-law, Jayda Rainey, thank you for your extraordinary and creative skills in the designing of my logo and book cover. God has blessed you with so many gifts and talents and my faith allows me to believe that He is well pleased with how you use your gifts to bless others.

To my dear friend, Michael "Pinball" Clemons, thank you for providing me with your invaluable insight into your own experience of becoming an author and speaker. I look forward to the day when you and I are on-stage and empowering others together.

To my best friend, Silisia Evans-Moses, thank you for introducing me to the Mary Kay business opportunity. Our journey to Mary Kay was divinely orchestrated and I am in definite belief that our future is brighter than ever!

Foreword

Pitfalls of Entrepreneurship is on recognizing, experiencing, and avoiding pitfalls to reaching the height of one's entrepreneurial spirit. It is a strong personal story of the author's life experiences from her first job to that of a successful entrepreneur. It deals with encouraging the inner desire to become an entrepreneur and the many challenges and risks that come with it.

This book offers ten pitfalls to avoid where possible and experience where needed on your way to becoming a successful entrepreneur. The author pulls from a series of business experiences and her faith to share insights important to understand when one embarks on the entrepreneurial journey. The purpose is to help the reader explore the possible pitfalls any prospective entrepreneur will encounter.

It is a way of thinking about potential pitfalls rather than a full review of entrepreneurship that is introduced here. We are reminded that making decisions to start entrepreneurial ventures can be difficult, but it is hoped that this book will assist those who have goals of becoming entrepreneurs to be successful in achieving their goals.

Pitfalls of Entrepreneurship is a good read for those seeking to become and are budding entrepreneurs. One will come away from this powerful story encouraged and inspired.

Joseph Smiley, Dean
Professor of Economics
St. Petersburg College

Introduction

I grew up in a family considered to be "middle class." My parent's combined income, during my childhood, was not six-figures, but we were not poor. I recall my parents applying for lunch aid while I attended elementary school. Lunch aid was a program where either the child's lunch was free or provided at a reduced cost. Apparently my parent's income level was too high to qualify for free or reduced lunch. I recall my mom saying, "Well, if we don't qualify for lunch aid, I don't know who qualifies for it." Nonetheless, neither I, nor my siblings, ever lacked. We lived in a small, 2-bedroom home with a carport. My parents owned a duplex apartment building that sat directly behind our main home. As long as I can remember, the duplex was always occupied by tenants. I didn't understand it at the time, but my parents actually owned property. I guess this was extra income, and looking back I am certain they did not have an accountant, financial advisor, or anyone to provide advice on how to maximize tax savings or even build a real estate empire. I grew up watching them go to work every day, collect rent from the tenants, pay the insurance lady who came by on a monthly basis, and I never once heard them talk about being their own bosses or entrepreneurship.

Another vivid memory of entrepreneurship came through my high school basketball coach, Larry Parks. Larry played an integral part in shaping my basketball skills and (although I was not aware of it at the time) giving me an example of business ownership. Larry and the Parks family owned several t-shirt and gift boutiques on Clearwater Beach. He also owned a printing press where many of the t-shirts sold in the boutiques were made. I worked for Larry part-time during my high school summers. Imagine that? Unaware at the time, I was given another up front example of entrepreneurship through my basketball coach.

Born in the 40s, my parents grew up in South Carolina in large sibling households (my mother is 1 of 6 and my dad is 1 of 9). I have heard many stories about the daily routines of each sibling, which were to attend school, return home to first do homework to ensure good grades, work out in the corn fields, complete household chores and attend church several times per week (and definitely on Sunday). This cycle repeated every week. My parents know the importance of hard work. This hard work was later displayed on each of their jobs, where they each worked, respectively, for the same company for over 30+ years. Success to them is in the form of retiring with a pension and/or 401k and then to live on that savings until our God calls them home. I am blessed to say that they are currently gainfully retired, and fortunately both of them worked during a time when companies actually contributed generously towards their pensions and 401k savings plans.

Born in October 1970, I am the oldest. My brother, Louis "Anthony" Evans, Jr. was born in May 1973, and my sister, Alicia Evans, was born in August 1979. We all excelled in sports, from little league through high school. Our gift of athleticism afforded my sister and me basketball scholarships to Florida Southern College. Athletic scholarships are only given to a small percentage of student athletes. What made my sister's and my scholarships so extraordinary is that we both received scholarships to attend the same college, playing for the same head coach, Norm Benn, exactly 9 years apart.

My brother died at the young age of 17. During his senior year in high school he collapsed during a normal basketball practice. Ironically, we both were in basketball practice at the same time. Anthony was at Clearwater High School, and I was at Florida Southern College. On that fateful day, February 7, 1991, I was pulled out of basketball practice to the news that he had collapsed, and after being revived twice he later died from an enlarged heart. I drove home from Lakeland, FL as fast as I could, thinking how I wasn't able to say goodbye, but grateful that at least he died doing something he loved. He was athletically gifted in two sports: as the quarterback in football and a power forward/center in basketball. Had he lived, I am certain he, too, would have been the recipient of an athletic scholarship.

Experiencing the thrill and excitement of earning a basketball scholarship taught me early that doing the things that most people won't rewards you with the things that most people will never receive. This continues to be true today. I tasted success at a young age and became accustomed to it. There were many summers I would have loved to hang out with my friends, but I participated in basketball camps to further my skills. I do recall very few times that I was able to hang out with friends, but they were few. Naturally, at the time it seemed unfair. However, the sacrifice was worth it, and I finished college in 1992 with no debt and a Bachelor of Science Degree in Financial Business Management.

At the time of reading this book, you may be gainfully employed working for someone else or unemployed. You may be at the contemplation stage of being your own boss, or you may have recently launched your own business. Then again, you may have had your own business for quite some time and still find yourself struggling in the pits of entrepreneurship as you will see described in this book. If you are in a pit, I encourage you to acknowledge where you are, but more importantly resolve to take action. God wants us all to lead prosperous lives. Like myself, you may have fallen into a pit (or two) on your journey. Pits are not all bad. Pits are actually opportunities. Pits provide the chance to exercise the power that God has given each of us to rise above adversity. One of the greatest biblical "pit experiences" that inspires me the most is in the book of Genesis. Joseph, son of Jacob and Rachel, had the innate ability to interpret dreams. His brothers were jealous of what they perceived to be favoritism towards Joseph. Joseph was destined for a "pit experience" the minute he told his brothers how, one day, they would bow down to him and he would rule the land. Can you see how sharing prematurely with others what God has given insight on only to you could possibly be a bad idea? As the story goes, Joseph was placed into an actual pit. Genesis 37:4 states, "When his brothers saw that their father loved him more than any of them, they hated him and could not speak a kind word to him." *New International Version.* Some people are not ready to accept or embrace your greatness. I encourage you to read Joseph's story in the book of Genesis beginning at Chapter 37. God had a plan for Joseph and he has a plan for each of us. Joseph's pit stop was all a part of God's plan for his life. No matter how far you've fallen, God can pick you up, restore you and set you back on the path he has specifically designed for you.

Pit 1 ~ Make Your Own Decisions or Someone Else Will

As a college graduate, the first one in my family, I had the same high expectations that most college graduates have: to graduate and secure employment within the field of my degree. Additionally, I expected to be paid a "high five-figure" income simply because of my college degree. My first real job was with Fortune Bank as a teller. Teller positions in 1992 were considered "entry level" in the banking industry, and entry level banking positions were not high five-figure income positions. I earned $24,000 annually and I realized quickly that although the college degree helped me earn more than a high school graduate, it did not guarantee a large salary. Nonetheless, I was excited to have a job and it was not long thereafter that I set my sights on "moving up" the corporate ladder.

After being in the banking industry for 3 years, news came that the banking company with which I was employed was going to be acquired by AmSouth Bank. Some of my coworkers were very concerned about the possibility of being replaced. Honestly, I was not that concerned. I knew there was a possibility that AmSouth could bring in their own associates to operate the bank the AmSouth way, but what could I do about it? Unbeknownst to me, this was an early use of the power of my mind and my ability to block out negative thinking. By the time of the acquisition, I had worked my way up to sitting at a desk performing duties as a Customer Service Representative. CSR's were the persons that handled the opening and closing of accounts, Certificates of Deposits, Money Markets, etc. Transitioning as a CSR was a bit more detailed than transitioning as a Teller. There were more system enhancements to learn and banking regulations of which to be aware. In the end, I retained my employment through the acquisition, although I was relocated to another AmSouth Bank branch within the Clearwater area.

Shortly after the acquisition and my relocation, I began to have thoughts of seeking other employment. I did not like the feeling of being at the mercy of someone else determining whether or not I would have a job. In reality, all employers in Florida have their employees at their mercy since Florida is an "at will" state. This means that either you or your employer can terminate your employment at any time and without advance notice, but the reason must be legal. I never discussed the thought of changing jobs with my parents. I did not share with them in what companies I was interested, or even why I desired to change jobs. Why? I decided that it was my life; thus, it was my decision. **Pit 1....Make Your Own Decisions or Someone Else Will.** I have learned that having discussions with people about decisions that I need to make in my life opens the door for their opinions. Opinions often interfere with what you need to do and they can cloud your judgment. Never seek advice or value the opinion of anyone whom you would not trade places. Don't get me wrong. I love my parents and admire their work ethic and their loyalty to the companies for which they worked, respectively. My father retired from the Pinellas Suncoast Transit Authority after 30 years and my mother retired from

Instrument Transformers after 34 years. However, this was now the 90's and jobs were in abundance. At the time, I did not embrace the philosophy of remaining with the same company for 30+ years while hoping that the value that I placed on myself would one day be represented by an equivalent salary. When I left the bank in 1995, I was earning approximately $30,000, which was not much more than when I started, and the amount certainly did not represent what I believed was my value.

Too often people ask others "what would you do" in this or that situation. The truth of the matter is they can't tell you what they would do. If they have not faced a similar decision or choice they can only guess at what they would do. I have learned that experience is what makes advice valuable and worth considering. At the end of the day, after prayer you must still make the best decision based upon where you are in life at that moment. Avoid the pit of making your decisions based solely or on the majority of someone else's opinion. If the decision you make ends of being a bad one, at least it's YOUR bad decision. Making my own decisions has continued to prove beneficial during my journey. Making a major, journey altering decision would later appear in my life, which you will discover as you continue to read this book.

"Don't ever make decisions based on fear. Make decisions based on hope and possibility. Make decisions based on what should happen, not what shouldn't."

~ Michelle Obama

Pit 2 ~ Doubting Your Inner Knowing

My corporate journey continued beyond the banking industry. After leaving AmSouth, I worked for three companies that each played an extremely pivotal role in my development of learning how to work with and lead others. I held the position of Internal Auditor with Pinch-a-Penny (Pool & Patio Supply Chain) from 1995 – 1998, an Internal Auditor with Rooms to Go from 1998 – 2001 and Financial Business Consultant with Cox Target Media from 2001 – 2005. Yes, I worked for three different companies over a 10 year period of time. Remember, I did not have a mindset of remaining with a company for 30+ years as my parents did. Jobs were in abundance during this time of my life and I was unafraid of change.

It was during my employment with each of these companies that I recognized how rare it was for an African-American female to have a position of leadership and authority. At both Pinch-A-Penny and Rooms to Go, I was the only African-American female auditor on a team of auditors. I was not raised as a child to see the color of someone's skin as a barrier. We are all God's children. However, naïve I was not. I knew that as a minority, I must exude excellence and professionalism.

As an auditor with Pinch-A-Penny, my role included review and analysis of a franchise owner's financial records. Most importantly, I was there to ensure that the sales totals from which their franchise fee was calculated actually reconciled with what was reported to the corporate office. Some may view an auditor as intimidating or even threatening. There is a misleading stigma surrounding the auditor's purpose and that is that auditors are there to "uncover" something being done wrong in the business or regarding the business finances. Although that can happen, I intentionally worked to create a new perspective on how each business owner regarded me and my purpose. As an auditor, I intentionally made the effort to treat my clients as I would want to be treated. I created an environment of positive energy, with my beautiful smile and warm greeting, from the moment I entered the building. I conducted my work in a timely manner (usually within 1 -2 days), and I was sure not to interfere with the owner's daily duties unless absolutely necessary. Additionally, I intentionally aimed to leave my clients with best practices tips that could be used to improve their business. These simple acts allowed me to create a favorable rapport with each business owner. Even in cases where my audit work brought forth correction and written reprimand, my clients respected me enough to accept the discovery and the instructions for correction.

What is an inner knowing? I define it as God's whisper. Sometimes the whisper is barely heard, but it is definite. When I made the decision to leave Pinch-A-Penny, it was not because of dissatisfaction with the company or my duties. I decided to pursue another opportunity for growth. Pinch-a-Penny was based out of Clearwater, and 90% of its stores were in Florida. Where else would a Pool & Patio Supply Chain thrive other than in the sunny state of Florida? There was a store or two in the states of Georgia and Tennessee. However, I heard God's whisper that he had another opportunity for me. Here is where some may fall into **Pit**

2……Doubting Your Inner Knowing. When an inner knowing arises within some question, ignore it, or debate it with God by asking him to give you a "sign." The fact that you recognized or felt the inner feeling actually *is the sign*. Oftentimes, people remain on a job or in relationships when they know they should move on. In my case with Pinch-A-Penny, I was not being prompted to move from a bad situation. I was transitioning because of an opportunity. Rooms to Go offered me the opportunity to hold another position of Internal Auditor; however, with travel in more states outside of Florida, Georgia and Tennessee, and my base salary went from $45,000 to $65,000. I remained with Rooms to Go for three wonderful years while obtaining additional valuable experience as an Internal Auditor. I traveled over 85% of my time and honestly enjoyed it. However, God whispered once again and I responded to the inner knowing that it was time to move on. My season was coming to an end.

Thus, in 2001, I carried my experience and work principles into a position as a Financial Business Consultant with Cox Target Media (CTM). Similar to my position of Internal Auditor with Pinch-A-Penny and Rooms to Go, I was on a team of other Financial Business Consultants. Pay attention to the pattern of positions that I held. Each of the three positions were leadership oriented within a team of other leaders. Working independently yet within a team with each company would prove to give immeasurable experience that I would later use as an entrepreneur. This was all God's divine plan. Does your work experience have a pattern? Do you see common threads that could very well show what you are most passionate about in life? Pay attention to the pattern and don't be afraid to make the move.

Each Financial Business Consultant was assigned a certain number of clients. It was during my employment with CTM that I truly acknowledged the pure joy of freedom and flexibility. I did have some freedom and flexibility with my prior two companies. However, with CTM, I acknowledged it and embraced it even more. There was something very empowering about being able to set my own work schedule, arrange my own travel schedule and manage my own expenses. Do you remember the feeling you had when you and your parents finally had all your belongings unloaded into your college dorm room or apartment and then they left campus for their return trip home? Yes, that feeling of freedom and flexibility.

As a Financial Business Consultant, I was responsible for the budgets, financial planning, debt reduction/elimination strategies and the improvement of gross profit for 15 franchise owners. CTM is the parent company of Valpak. Most people know Valpak by the coupons that arrive via mail in the infamous blue envelope. Well, my clients were some of those Valpak franchise owners. Thus, my consulting services were provided to entrepreneurs. Imagine that? I was now in a position to give business advice, complete financial budgets and provide debt reduction strategies to those who owned their own business. When they operated their business efficiently, and most importantly, at profit level, CTM experienced greater profits.

With my clients located in various cities within the United States, I was able to experience even more travel all over the United States. Our team of Financial Business Consultants worked together, and at times traveled together. We all reported directly to one of three Vice Presidents until a manager was hired during my second year with the company. This new manager became the person to whom we directly reported and it was clear (at least to me) that this was not a good decision. His personality did not fit in at all with the team. We were all outgoing, independent, fun and interactive. He was introverted, reserved, all business, straightforward, rigid and he lacked any sense of humor. Our VP's were more "hands off" and the new manager wanted to be "hands on." I compared this change to when the news came of the merger during my time in banking. The change was not welcomed, but apparently our VP's recognized the need to release themselves from this area of responsibility. After a few meetings with our new manager it became evident that he was given the position for his prior financial management experience and not his people management experience. Unfortunately, when you work for someone else you have no opinion on who should be hired. I did not know this then; however, my new manager provided me with the first glimpse of who I did not want to be if I was ever given the responsibility of managing a team.

Nevertheless, I took the new manager and his lack of people management ability in stride. After all, I could not change the decision. I could only control how I responded to the decision. Thus, I made the decision to continue to perform my duties as remarkably as I had become known for. I accepted the fact that I would have to interact with our new manager, and when those times arose, my work would speak for itself. I realized early in my professional career that there was something satisfying, and even empowering, when I held on to my power. I am not referencing the type of power that is apparent with a person in a position of authority. I am referring to the type of mental power that you and I own. Often times it is our mental power that we give away to situations, circumstances and even people. We may not be able to predict and control every circumstance; however, we always have the power to control our attitude towards it.

There came a moment in late 2004 while sitting at home on a Sunday afternoon when I could literally hear another inner whisper. I cannot recall the exact reason as to why my future was on my mind, but it was. Although my manager would never be someone I would invite to dinner, I did not dislike him. This inner whisper was different. It was not guiding me into a direction of moving to pursue employment at another company. For the first time I believe that I heard God's whisper saying, "I have prepared you and it is time to be your own boss." Sadly, I had to endure the perils of another pit before taking action into the direction of God's plan for my life.

"An inner knowing, along with a burning desire, is the prerequisite for becoming a person capable of manifesting his or her heart's desires."

~ Wayne Dyer

Pit 3 ~ A Comfort Zone

What? Be my own boss? Become an entrepreneur? Why would I want to do that? There are ideas that are good; there are ideas that are bad; then there are ideas that are God ideas. Becoming an entrepreneur was certainly a God idea. God ideas require people to take action in faith. Up until that moment in 2004, I only had childhood discussions about having my own business. My best friend and first cousin, Silisia, and I would talk about having our own business. Her father, my uncle, owned a store. It was simply called "The Corner Store" because it sat at the corner of the road. In today's time, his store would be the equivalent of a 7-11. The corner store had snacks, drinks, video games and a pool table. My brother and I would visit their family in South Carolina during the summer and on many days we would spend the entire day at my uncle's store. This visual of business ownership through this store was similar to the visual of rental property ownership displayed years ago by my parents. Silisia and I did not discuss with our parents what business ownership was all about; we simply watched them model it. I don't even think we knew exactly what we wanted to do. However, we did innocently talk about some type of business that we would eventually operate together. Imagine that? She at the time lived in South Carolina, and I lived in Florida. Yet, during our early teenage years we discussed having a business together and God saw to it that these childhood discussions would actually become reality in our lives. Words do have power!

In my position with CTM, through raises and my travel package, I earned a great six-figure income, worked with clients that I was able to assist in maintaining or becoming profitable businesses, traveled the country and aside from having a manager with no congenial personality, I had an enormous amount of freedom and flexibility. From my vantage point and that of my family, I was successful. Thus, why would I, or anyone, want to do anything different? Even though I had absolutely no experience in operating my own business I did possess a very extensive amount of experience in working with business owners. My education in Financial Business Management coupled with my professional work experience to date was all God's plan in his preparation for me to be my own boss. God's latest whisper that I should step out and become my own boss went against the familiarity of what was already established in my life (respect from others, a managerial position, steady income, an adequate lifestyle, continuous travel). Unintentionally, I had fallen into **Pit 3.....A Comfort Zone.**

Comfort is simply a feeling of contentment. Contentment represents a place of satisfaction. A comfort zone is a situation where someone feels safe and at ease, and it is a settled method of working that requires little effort. Considering my income, position and the travel across the country, I can admit that I was in a comfort zone. A challenge within a client's financial performance would occasionally arise; however, I certainly found ease in my responsibilities. Naturally, I did not identify it as a comfort zone, but that is exactly what it was. Being in a comfort zone at different times in life may not have been bad...unless the comfort zone turns into a pit. Despite my contentment, I could still hear God. Have you ever heard from God yet decided that it is not him? It is not the right time? Or, you look at the current circumstances and rationalize that you are good right where you are? There are many excuses that one may tend to make when the time to move forward is evident.

Some will remain in a comfort zone out of fear. Fear of change. Fear of the unknown. Fear of failure. Fear of success. Fear of disappointing others. Fear of being all that God has called you to be. There are many different reasons why some will choose to remain in this pit either permanently or, at the very least, too long. Here are a few warning phrases that may indicate you are in Pit 3 - A Comfort Zone:

1. I can't leave this job and start my own business. What about insurance?

2. I have seen too many people in my family fail.

3. I know exactly how much money I will earn each week/month. Why exchange definite income for uncertain income?

4. I have been in my position/at this company for over 10 years. Why would I want to take a chance and do anything else different?

5. I don't know anything about operating my own business.

6. What if that's not God speaking to me?

7. What will my friends think/say?

8. I am not good enough to step out on my own.

9. I don't have enough money to start my own business.

10. I don't have enough time to start my own business.

If you have ever stated or pondered any of the above statements, you are, or most likely have been, in Pit 3. Great things never come from comfort zones. One of the hardest decisions one may ever make is leaving a comfort zone. It can be scary and intimidating. However, I encourage you to never allow Pit 3 to overshadow the knowing of when it is time to pursue other opportunities. Joshua 1:9 states, "Have not I commanded you? Be strong and courageous. Do not be afraid; do not be discouraged; for the Lord your God will be with you wherever you go." *New International Version*. Simply stated, God is with each of us anywhere we go. Choosing to leave a comfort zone requires a greater trust and an expanded faith. Once I realized that I could not remain in my comfort zone, the alignment of my life's journey eventually collided with the unknown territory of entrepreneurship.

"The Three C's of Life: Choices, Chances, Changes. You must make a Choice to take a Chance or your life will never Change."

~ Zig Ziglar

Pit 4 ~ God's Divine Timing

In 2001, Silisia, launched her own business as a Mary Kay Independent Beauty Consultant. She had tried a few other home-based businesses. In one business, she sold a conglomerate of products ranging from home cleaning products to vitamins and other personal goods. As consultant in her second business, she sold jewelry. She never approached me with the opportunity to join her in either of those businesses. However, the Mary Kay opportunity proved to be different. She experienced early success. One of her most notable early successes was earning her first Mary Kay career car 7 weeks from the day she started the business. As I would later come to discover, earning a Mary Kay Career Car is a huge accomplishment and doing so in 7 weeks is absolutely astounding.

While working as a Computer Science Engineer and also earning a great six-figure income, she worked her Mary Kay business part-time. Even from a distance I could tell she enjoyed the business because I would hear about the travel, business conferences, the extra income that she was earning and the fun she was experiencing with other successful Mary Kay business owners. However, my very narrow view of a Mary Kay business extended only to cosmetics, which I did not wear. Remember, I was a successful professional in my own right and there was no way Mary Kay, a cosmetics company, could be for me. It is here that many people turn a blind eye to what could be an opportunity that leads them to the realization of the lifestyle of their dreams. Our childhood dream of being entrepreneurs was not meant to begin in her first two attempts at other home-based businesses. Why? I truly believe it was because God did not prompt her to share them with me. On the other hand, he did prompt her to share the Mary Kay opportunity with me. Yet, even in her first approach for me to join her, which came in 2002, I turned a blind eye to the notion of owning my own Mary Kay business and dismissed her invitation. In fact, I dismissed it until 2004. Keep in mind that I believe God whispered to me in 2004, not 2002. If God did whisper to me in 2002, I can look back and admit that I emphatically ignored Him.

Through 2004, I continued my work as a Financial Business Consultant for CTM. Over that timeframe, I assisted my clients in reducing debt, becoming sound business owners, developing yearly financial plans and more. In other words, my clients were succeeding and I was an integral part of their success. Silisia continued to work her corporate job while building her business as an Independent Beauty Consultant by sharing the products and the opportunity. Ironically, in 2002, after the first invitation and my decline to join her, our relationship became strained. My life as a corporate employee had not seen anything outside of being a corporate employee. With her increasing love for her Mary Kay business, our conversations became different. Make no mistake - I was happy for her. However, I could not relate to what she was doing and because I did not wear makeup my support in buying the products was very limited. The one foundation that I purchased was not the right shade, and even if it had been the right shade, I was not going to wear it, anyway. It seemed as if we had nothing in common anymore. Although we both were traveling the country, I was traveling on behalf of a company that I worked for and she was traveling on behalf of her own business. We spoke about our successes to each other; however, our success occurred in two entirely different arenas. The blessing of it all was although we experienced less communication we remained in touch. Our love for each other never diminished and our dreams of being business owners together never died.

Eventually, I realized that I was in **Pit 4…..God's Divine Timing**. God and his divine timing brought the opportunity that was given to Silisia in 2001 to me in 2004. This pit is necessary. In other words, it is a God-ordained pit. If there is such a thing as a good pit, this would be it. Truthfully, this is a pit that allows God to be God because his timing is perfect. Sometimes we overlook this pit and God allows us to go around the mountain until we realize the error of our ways. Pit 4 allows us the chance to elevate our trust and faith in Him. Most pits we fall into are of our own volition. On the contrary, Pit 4 is God's planned pit because it is continual. Everything that occurs in life occurs in God's timing. Jeremiah 29:11 states, "For I know the plans that I have for you, declares the Lord, plans to prosper you and not to harm you, plans to give you hope and a future." *New International Version*. Simply stated, God has a plan for each of us to prosper, be successful and live abundant lives before we are even born. His timing is absolutely and always perfect. Even though the business I would eventually launch was given to my best friend in 2001, God knew that it would take me three years to step into it.

While navigating through the conclusion of a bad relationship, I decided to get away. I used some of my vacation time to travel to Houston, TX to meet up with Silisia. She was there on yet another Mary Kay business trip called "Fall Advance." By this time, she had eclipsed the position of Mary Kay Independent Sales Director, which I would later came to understand represents the Top 2% of the entire Mary Kay independent sales force. I did not mind traveling to Houston because with all of my corporate travel, I had enough mileage for a free airline ticket and Silisia advised that I could stay with her. A free airline ticket and hotel stay? Sign me up. Honestly, I simply wanted to see my best friend. God's Pit 4 plan was progressing exactly as He destined it to unveil. It was a win-win situation. She now had an opportunity to expose me to her world of Mary Kay and I had a chance to get away and spend a little time with my best friend. Silisia shared her itinerary for the conference, when she would be unavailable and when we would have time to spend together. I was already accustomed to traveling and maneuvering throughout any city. Thus, I simply planned my visit to the mall, various restaurants and other points of interest while she would be in session.

While in Houston, I felt as if someone was slowly releasing air out of a balloon. It was a tremendous relief to embrace her, laugh with her, dine with her and simply enjoy fruitful conversation. We finally had the ability to catch up on what was going on in each other's lives. For the first time in years our time spent together was similar to our childhood times together. Simple. Fun. No charades. Innocent conversation. Genuine care and concern. The trip merged our lives onto the same road once again.

On the second to the final night of my stay she obtained permission from her National Sales Director for me to sit in on one of the main events of the conference. This was significant for various reasons:

1. Someone who was not a Mary Kay Independent Beauty Consultant is typically not allowed entrance into these events.

2. Silisia wanted me to see, up close and personal, the culture and environment that she and other Mary Kay Independent Beauty Consultants enjoyed.

3. My presence would generate questions about the opportunity that she would be more than happy to answer.

I attended the event and was completely amazed. Impressed. In awe, actually. Over my corporate career I had been to various business conferences, workshops and seminars. However, I had never witnessed the type of energy, celebration of achievement and outward acknowledgement of God. I recognized almost instantly why Silisia was thriving successfully with her business. The event was packed with success testimonies, recognition, love, glitz and glamour, but most importantly, it had my best friend.

At the end of the night, I was introduced directly to Silisia's National Sales Director. She greeted me and then said, "Is this the sister that you have been talking about having as your business partner?" Silisia replied, "Yes." The National Sales Director then focused her attention back to me and asked, "Well, what are you waiting for?" and moved on to greet the next person waiting to speak with her. Silisia let me know that she would meet me back in our hotel room, but I knew from that encounter that becoming a Mary Kay

Independent Beauty Consultant was the business that I was destined to launch. The alignment of my life's journey collided into the unknown territory of entrepreneurship beginning January 2005.

"You can either build the future and fortune of someone else or you can build your own future and fortune. There is a difference."

~ Andrea D. Evans-Dixon

Pit 5 ~ Discussing Major League Decisions with Minor League Thinkers

My best friend was ecstatic. We were finally in business together as we so often discussed when we were younger. I was excited. It was something new and it gave me a new challenge. Becoming an entrepreneur as a Mary Kay Independent Beauty Consultant was unlike anything I had done in my adult life. After all, I knew absolutely nothing about skin care and cosmetics. I suffered from severe eczema most of my adult life and the Classic Basic Skin Care System by Mary Kay (which my best friend gifted to me while in Houston) was the only skin care regimen I had ever used. My skin was accustomed to topical lotions and creams prescribed by my dermatologist. Needless to say, I was thrilled beyond measure at the way my skin was responding to the regimen. After three months of using the products the eczema had totally cleared, and for the first time I was excited to attend my quarterly appointment with my dermatologist. This personal testimony of my own skin was my sole selling tool of the skin care products. Years of brand-named lotions and creams recommended from the dermatologist were all topped in three months by consistent use of a basic cleanser, moisturizer, toner and a mask.

What about the Mary Kay business? What was I going to do with my business while still working 50 – 60 hours per week? I decided to do what I had done my entire career: excel and provide my clients with top-notch service. It did not matter that I was now in the skin care and cosmetics industry. My clients deserved the best service I could provide and I knew how to do that. Even while in the early stages of my Mary Kay business, I thought it a good idea to make an attempt to have to my own financial consulting business. After all, I had been performing the duties of a financial budgeting consultant for a corporate company. Now that I was discovering entrepreneurship, why not obtain my own clients who could use my services to help them better manage their business? Thus, I decided that I would launch two businesses. That was not God's plan. During the same time as I obtained a contract with five business owners for my consulting services, God allowed me the opportunity to experience success within my Mary Kay business. The rewards and gratification within my Mary Kay business far outweighed those I was experiencing with my financial business clients. The same way that I learned how to take care of my skin, I taught others to do the same. It did not take long for me to realize it was not meant for me to have a business performing the duties I did on my corporate job. In this case, it was not failure in my consulting business. It was simply God's way of shining a brighter light on the path that he intended for me. That path was to build a successful Mary Kay business.

I asked my best friend and (now) Director how to earn $300 - $400 profit per month. She happily helped me devise a strategy that would work within my travel schedule, and I consistently operated my business 4 – 5 hours per week. Although I was what I considered "busy," I still found the time to give t0 my new business. Remember the early achievements I shared that my best friend experienced in

2001? Well, she shared her success strategies with me. Imagine that? I was able to benefit from the experiences she learned, hurdles she overcame and techniques she used in building her business. I wondered: had I gone into my boss's office and asked him to give me instruction on how to do what he does with the intent of being in his position, would he have openly and willingly shared those strategies? Nonetheless, my consistency over a short seven month period, willingness to follow her lead and a desire for greatness provided me with successful results as well. With the extra income, I was able to pay off my car, an Acura 3.2 TL, enter into a qualification period to become an Independent Sales Director and earn my first Mary Kay Career Car (to name a few).

After earning the first career car in July 2005, and traveling to my first Mary Kay Seminar that same month, I decided to take another vacation. This vacation was my first consecutive two weeks of time off ever. Not once had I ever found the need to take two consecutive weeks off of work until July 2005. I needed the time to seek God's guidance on what I had been pondering about my Mary Kay business. This was a major, life altering decision. I began my business, but God did not mention anything to me about leaving my corporate job. Yet, I was actually having thoughts of leaving my corporate job. The experience and satisfaction of making women feel and look beautiful, as well as helping some of them launch their own businesses, was unexplainable. Only God could provide me with the clarity of what I needed to do.

Although I spent time doing two of my favorite hobbies, shopping and reading, my vacation was primarily spent at home. I spent quite a bit of time quietly in my home praying and listening. I was waiting on God to give me that whisper he had so clearly given me in the past when it was time to make a move. God did not whisper to me. I never doubted that He heard me. It was simply that He was not answering. Allow me to introduce you to and warn you about **Pit 5…..Discussing Major League Decisions with Minor League Thinkers**. This pit is dangerous because everyone has an opinion. My consideration of leaving my full-time corporate career to pursue and expand my Mary Kay business on a full-time basis was major. It meant reviewing my finances, personal spending and more. Anytime one is making a decision that could possibly constitute a lifestyle change is major. Often times when one is not receiving an answer or confirmation in what is believed to be a timely manner they can be led to seek answers from friends or family. I consider minor league thinkers as those who:

1. Accept the status quo.

2. Impose their limiting beliefs upon you.

3. Offer advice without experience or first-hand knowledge.

4. Voice their doubt and impose their fear from personal failure upon you.

5. Don't see themselves doing anything more than what they are doing presently.

Falling into Pit 5 can cause one to doubt his/her own power or ability to make his/her own decisions, and I did not want to openly invite doubt into my mind. Thus, I told no one. I chose not to discuss anything about what I was considering for my business. My best friend, the one who introduced the Mary Kay business to me, did not know. My parents did not know. My parents did not even know that I had earned the first career car. Leaving my corporate career after 13 years was exciting and daunting all at the same time. I could see the added flexibility in my life, but I could not see how I was going to graduate to the income that I had become accustomed to from my corporate career. There were moments when I could not wrap my mind around the fact that I was considering conducting my business as a full-time entrepreneur. With my education and work experience, it would have been a natural transition for me to launch my own business as an Independent Financial and Budgeting Consultant, but I did not.

At the conclusion of my two-week vacation, I took the largest faith leap in my entire life. I want to make it known that I never received that "go ahead" whisper from God. This time, I decided to listen to what I was not hearing and believe that if I was making the wrong decision I would have some type of bad feeling. God would never fail me. I believed that God decided to advise me in reverse. What does that mean? If He was not going to give me the green light to leave my job, He would give me some type of physical sign (a bad headache, upset stomach, or something). Nothing happened. I spoke to no one about my decision. I returned to work and submitted my two-week notice of resignation. My last day was scheduled for August 5, 2005. I was leaving my corporate career within 8 months of launching my business.

While serving out my two-week notice, here is what happened:

1. I shared the decision with my best friend and Director, Silisia. She was genuinely happy for me, and my decision gave her the inspiration to leave her full-time career as a Computer Science Engineer.

2. I finished my qualification and earned the esteemed position of a Mary Kay Independent Sales Director. The Successful Divas Unit was born. Since I had always viewed myself as an achiever, I coined the word Diva to represent Dynamic Independent Victorious Achiever.

3. Becoming an Independent Sales Director placed me in the Top 2% of the entire Mary Kay Independent Sales Force.

4. I positioned myself to earn the 2nd Mary Kay Career Car.

During those two weeks, God winked at me in the spirit. Those achievements were essentially assurances that I made the correct decision in becoming a full-time entrepreneur. It was not until the Thursday prior to the final Friday of my two-week notice that I advised my mother that I was leaving my corporate career to pursue my Mary Kay business on a full-time basis. She was appalled and did not believe me. This did not surprise me and it was one of the main reasons why I did not share nor seek her advice on the decision. The next few phrases that she expressed were expressions of both fear on her part and concern for my well-being. She asked, "I thought you were only doing Mary Kay part-time?" "How are you going to pay your bills?" "What if they (the company, Mary Kay Inc.) come and take your car back?" "Why would you want to leave your full-time, well-paying, corporate career to sell lipstick?" It was evident that it was time for me to share with my mother that I had already earned not one, but two cars, and I provided her insight on how the Mary Kay Career Car program worked. Additionally, I advised her that I had become an Independent Sales Director and what this career level meant in the world of Mary Kay. Upon conclusion of our conversation, she was not fully at ease; however, she knew her daughter. I would never make a decision without prayer and a plan.

Needless to say, there was no turning back. I am grateful that I did not subject myself to those questions prior to turning in my two-week notice of resignation. Essentially, I eluded Pit 5 and you can, too. I discovered that God had already divinely downloaded everything I needed. He equipped and prepared me for that moment, that decision, that distinctive opportunity to rely upon the peace of God that covered me that day I returned to work from vacation. Major league decisions require major league faith. When you have to make a decision into which only God (and your spouse, if married) should have input, then trust that He will never lead you astray. James 1:5 states, "If any of you lacks wisdom, you should ask God, who gives generously to all without finding fault, and it will be given to you." *New International Version.* After all, the biggest risk in life is choosing not to take a risk. I chose to take a risk on ME!

"The chances you take, the people you meet, the people you love, the faith that you have. That's what's going to define you."

~ Denzel Washington

Pit 6 ~ Refusing to Learn the Art of Saying 'No'

One of the first things that becoming an entrepreneur brought into my life was the reality that I was now my own boss. Was I nervous? Yes. Had I taken a leap of faith? Absolutely. My accountability was owed to no one else but me. The first week of being a full-time entrepreneur was exhilarating. I can recall sleeping in on that Monday, August 8, 2005. When I rose out of bed after 9:30 am that day, I remember thinking, "I sure won't be able to do this every day, but this sure feels great!"

One of the most critical components to experiencing success is setting goals. Goals are necessary in business, school, sports and in life overall. Goals provide a target, give direction and help one to measure success. Without a goal, one may find oneself operating without aim and running in circles. When I set my first goal in my Mary Kay business to earn $300 - $400 profit per month, I became laser focused on the activity required to generate the sales that would thereby produce the profit I desired. Even before transitioning into being my own boss, I understood that I must have an even greater commitment and discipline to achieve my goals. Why? The goal(s) that I once set as a part-time entrepreneur were no longer suitable to meet my life as a full-time entrepreneur. As a Mary Kay Independent Sales Director, I no longer had the luxury of developing and pursuing my personal goals only. Directorship involved the leading of others. There were now goals for my unit, which was comprised of women who had also decided to launch their own Mary Kay business and follow my leadership. Luke 12:48 states, "From everyone who has been given much, much will be demanded; and from the one who has been entrusted with much, much more will be asked." *New International Version.*

There are some individuals within two groups of people that typically do not understand what becoming an entrepreneur really means, especially if these individuals have never been an entrepreneur themselves (remember Pit 5). These individuals are commonly known as family and friends. When I worked at my corporate job, there was a job schedule outlined by hours. For the most part, I could accept invitations to birthday parties, lunch/ dinner dates, galas, the movies and various other events that were of interest to me. Because I held a position that paid me a set salary, I could spend an entire weekend doing absolutely nothing if I so desired. In launching my own business, there was a new way of earning income and it was called "commissions." A commission is an amount of money given as a percentage of value. My commission from the sale of the products in my business was 50% of the retail value. However, I also earned a commission based upon my ability to lead and guide others to success. As an entrepreneur, this meant that I was my business' greatest asset. Since it all hinged on me, I could no longer accept every invitation I received. This means I had to learn the art of saying 'no' without explaining myself. The word 'no' is actually a complete sentence. It does not require justification or explanation.

Welcome to **Pit 6……..Refusing to Learn the Art of Saying 'No.'** It took quite some time for me to learn the art of saying 'no,' and you will discover later in this chapter one of the most memorable times that I was tested on saying 'no'. The invitations that I could more easily accept from friends and family could not be accepted as easily once I became my own boss. Why? At times these engagements were held during the times that I had to operate my business. For example, I declined going to see a movie in the middle of the day on a Saturday because of a scheduled skin care party. On occasion, I declined going to dinner with friends on a Friday evening because of a commitment that I made to be present at an event hosted by a consultant within my unit. My support of a consultant in helping to reach her/his goals was an important aspect of my business. There were times when my friends would make comments such as "Andrea won't be going with us because she probably has some Mary Kay thing to do." What I realized was that many people want success in various areas of their lives; however, they are unwilling to change the things necessary or do things differently to experience success. Success is never by chance. Success is never convenient. On the contrary, success is intentional. There were countless phone calls that I opted out of answering because it became easier to not answer rather than having to say 'no.' Thus, I simply said, "No, I will not answer that call." With ongoing success, it became much easier to make the decisions that I was certain would benefit the advancement of my business. Why? I realized that I was doing something that many of my friends were not doing. I chose to have the discipline to do the things that my family and friends were not willing to do so that I could live a lifestyle that they probably never would. My ability to lead others, while building and sustaining a healthy customer database, brought on the rewards of not one, not two, but three Mary Kay Career Cars within 15 months of starting of my business. Yes, by March 2006, my unit and I were awarded the most prestigious car in Mary Kay's Career Car Program, the Pink Cadillac. The Cadillac was a visual representation of the work that my unit and I put into selling the Mary Kay products, as well as sharing the Mary Kay business opportunity. None of my family and friends, other than Silisia, operated a business, and most of them were still doing what they had been doing for years.

In my early days of learning to say 'no' to others, it seemed that I would miss something if I were not present. You may feel this way as well. It could take some time to rid your mind of the thoughts of what you could be doing rather than building your business. However, I encourage you to learn how to say 'no' and avoid Pit 6 if at all possible. On the other hand, should you fall into this pit, make a decision and take the necessary action-steps to exit quickly. Why? Failing to gracefully decline invitations will inevitably interfere with your growth. There is no one that has more to lose from a business than the owner. The opposite is also true. The owner has more to gain. As an entrepreneur, I am the boss. Most of my friends and family have a boss. I set my own schedule. Most of my friends and family work a set schedule. I go on vacation at my discretion. Most of my friends and family must take a vacation at the discretion of their boss. These differences are certainly not being shared to place a negative light upon anyone who chooses to work for someone else rather than themselves. I believe that recognizing these differences has helped me and will help you accept the fact that saying 'no' is a necessary duty if you want to build a successful business and live a lifestyle different from most.

Events, movies, dinners and lunch invitations were not the only things to which I had to learn when to say 'yes' and when to say 'no.' One of the most memorable and pivotal times in my entrepreneurial career occurred when I had to make a decision between traveling to Jamaica and continuing to build my business. In 2004, a good friend and I planned a vacation to an all-inclusive island in Jamaica. We were co-workers at Cox Target Media. Once plans were in place, we faithfully followed a payment plan and we both, not knowing we would need it, purchased travel insurance. As you discovered by reading Pit 5, as 2004 came to an end, I was preparing to launch my Mary Kay business. I did not know this when we began our plans for travel to Jamaica, but our trip was scheduled to occur during the same month that I was finishing the qualifications of becoming a Mary Kay Independent Sales Director. My friend and co-worker, who by this time had also launched her own Mary Kay business within my unit, questioned if we were still going to travel to Jamaica. Naturally, I wanted to go and so did she. However, I knew that there were several good reasons that I should not take the trip.

1. It was still within the first 8 months of owning my business.

2. Finishing Director Qualifications would place me in the top 2% of the Mary Kay Independent Sales Force.

3. I had already earned one Mary Kay Career Car and was within 60 days of earning the second one.

4. I had recently given my resignation to leave my corporate job.

5. I had begun earning commissionable income versus a customary salary.

I spoke with my best friend and Senior Director, Silisia. She provided her input, which included a few of her own personal experiences regarding decisions such as these and the impact it had on her business. What I loved about Silisia's input was that it provided realistic insight from two vantage points: 1) as my Senior Director in business, and 2) as my best friend. At the end of the conversation, she let it be known that it was my decision to travel to Jamaica or not. After another week, my friend directly asked, "Andrea, are we still going to Jamaica?" My reply was "no." Surprisingly, she agreed. I was not aware of this, but she desired to leave Cox Target Media as well and pursue her business as an entrepreneur. Not going to Jamaica would not only save money, but it would allow her (and me) the opportunity to continue working our businesses. I had inspired her to become an Independent Sales Director, and the time away would have caused us both to lose momentum in our businesses, individually and collectively. Only God knew at the time that we would need to use our travel insurance. We were able to obtain a refund and I am certain that had I chosen to go on the trip, the road through my first year as an entrepreneur would have been altered.

A decision to say 'yes' or 'no' is like coming to a fork in the road. One can either go right or left. Yes or no. Forks in the road give us the opportunity to build our faith. Only God knows our complete life. Since we are not privy to this information, we must trust our instinct, intuition, inner-knowing, God-given desires and, most importantly, we must trust God. Entrepreneurs must find a way to eliminate the distractions and unnecessary noise, ignore naysayers and not be concerned about what others are doing. The first 5 years of operating a business are crucial. In some cases, a business does not survive the first 5 years. Thus, the more disciplined one can be in the early years of operation, the better the chances are of developing good business practices and productive daily habits. This may seem like a hard task in the beginning, but give yourself permission to say 'no.'

"You have to decide what your highest priorities are and have the courage - pleasantly, smilingly, non-apologetically - to say 'no' to other things. And the way to do that is by having a bigger 'yes' burning inside."

~ Stephen Covey

Pit 7 ~ Managing Your Success with God as the Co-Pilot

I was raised in the church. My parents ensured my attendance in church every Sunday and my involvement in all youth activities. My mother was the Young People's Department Director at the church. My parents were and still are actively engaged today in our local church. Honestly, I can say that I have known *of* God and his son, Jesus Christ, as early as an elementary age simply from attending church. I learned how to pray and I even understood that prayer had power. As a teenager in high school, I recall one Sunday when I accepted the invitation for Jesus Christ to come into my life. My youth days were over. I believed the scripture that Jesus Christ died for my sins, was buried, and that on the third day after his burial, he was raised from the dead.

Knowing of Jesus Christ is totally different from having a relationship with Him. As any relationship develops, the persons involved spend time getting to know each other. Over time through my new found purpose in studying God's word, I discovered much more about the proper way to live, how to honor Him and His promises for my life. One of the main things that I learned early in my new relationship with Jesus Christ is that there was nothing I could do to "earn" His love. He loves me. Period. He desires to bless me abundantly. Period. His plan for my life is prosperity and success. Period. By the time I truly sought out a relationship with Jesus Christ, He had already done so much for me. I gained a better understanding of the phrase that I sometimes heard in a prayer: "Even if I had 10,000 tongues, I couldn't thank you enough." Long before my absolute dependence upon Him, my life was filled with blessings that I could not count even if I tried.

As is the case sometimes within many relationships, the excitement fades. One may tend not to place as much effort into making it thrive. I can truly admit that during my college years and the early days of my corporate career, my personal effort to nurture my relationship with Jesus Christ had weakened. As He is, was and always will be present. However, because He gives us free choice, He waits. As an adult, I never forgot my church roots. On the other hand, because of my relationship with Jesus Christ, attending church was no longer enough. My relationship with Him required that I acknowledge His presence and allow Him to direct my path.

Maybe you have heard the saying, "God is my co-pilot." What is a co-pilot? Merriam Webster defines co-pilot as "a qualified pilot who assists or relieves the pilot *but is not in command*." In other words, the co-pilot is not in authority. The co-pilot is not the lead pilot.

Within the first 15 months of owning my Mary Kay business, I experienced what some would consider an enormous amount of success. Here's what happened:

1. January 2005 ~ Launched Mary Kay business (part-time)

2. July 2005 ~ Earned the first Mary Kay Career Car (Pontiac Vibe)

3. August 2005 ~ Became a Mary Kay Independent Sales Director

4. August 2005 ~ Left my full-time, six-figure corporate career

5. September 2005 ~ Earned the second Mary Kay Career Car (Pontiac Grand Prix)

6. March 2006 ~ Earned the third Mary Kay Career Car (1st Pink Cadillac)

By March 2006, God had shown tremendous favor to my business and me. My 100% commission-based income was steadily increasing, and the number of consultants who decided to follow my leadership and join me in owning their own business had grown from one in February 2005 to over 100. The year 2006 would represent my first full year in business as an Independent Sales Director. Based upon my business's momentum I had no doubt that I would successfully reach and/or surpass the six-figure amount of income that I was earning on my corporate job prior to my departure. In all the years of going to church, then finally accepting Jesus Christ as my Savior, and even better developing a relationship with Jesus Christ, I discovered that I was in **Pit 7….. Managing Your (my) Success With God as the Co-Pilot**.

By the end of 2006 and into 2007, the number of consultants that I was leading as business owners had grown to over 100. At least three of those consultants followed my example and became Mary Kay Independent Sales Directors. Additionally, there were a few others who were in the qualifications process. I wish I could share with you that I sought the kingdom and His righteousness first each day. I had a good prayer life, God was enlarging my territory, and I was in a beautiful relationship with a man whom I was preparing to marry in May 2007. Yet, when I reflect upon my daily routine, when and how I included God, and in some cases, excluded Him in the operation my business, there is absolutely no comparison to how devoted I am to Godly living today. I have come to realize that I must seek Him first and be intentional on beginning, experiencing the day and completing each day with Him. I did not take the time to truly appreciate God for what He was doing in my business. Below are a few tendencies that have been evident in my life and business when God has been my Co-Pilot versus God being my Pilot:

God as my Co-Pilot (then)	God as my Pilot (now)
Unfaithful Tither	Faithful Tither
Operated my business by grinding	Operating my business with God's grace
Prayed after my day begins	Pray before my feet touch the floor
Gave thanks for the good outcomes	Give thanks for everything
Made plans without seeking guidance	Seek God's guidance first in all plans
Believed all were self-starters	Realize that some need encouragement
Invited God in when seeking a high achievement	Invite God in for all achievements (big or small)
Believed I could make things happen	Recognize that without Him nothing is possible
Achievement driven	Kingdom driven
Believed that I was in competition with others	Competition does not exist
Prayers filled with personal requests	Prayers asking what can I do for His glory
Insisted that others have big goals (like me)	Allow others to perform where they are content
Relied upon my own ideas	Seek God-inspired ideas
Implemented business activities & strategies that other Directors use in their business	Ask God, "Is this a strategy that I should implement?" or "Which strategy I should use?"
Occasionally paused to communicate with God throughout the day	Intentionally create time to meditate, pray and express thanks throughout the day

Business in competition with others   Business for God's glory

God desires to be a part of every area of our lives. There is absolutely nothing too hard, big, small, high, or low for God. He will never force his way in. The choice is and will always be ours. However, make no mistake about it - we are all created to fulfill God's purpose for our lives, not our own agendas. When we are not living or operating in agreement with His purpose, He has a way to get our attention. One of the very first books of the bible that resonated with me as an entrepreneur is Deuteronomy. Blessings and curses are set before each of us and we must daily choose life. When we obey, serve and seek God first in everything, blessings and wealth are promised as they were to Moses and the Israelites. Deuteronomy 8:17-18 states, "You may say to yourself, 'My power and the strength of my hands have produced this wealth for me.' But remember the Lord your God, for it is He who gives you the ability to produce wealth, and so confirms his covenant, which he swore to your ancestors, as it is today." *New International Version.* These verses clearly advise that God is the pilot. The book of Deuteronomy outlines many of His promises and it shows our never-ending need for God in our everyday lives…both personal and business.

Being an entrepreneur is a divine assignment for me. His purpose for me (and you) includes the development of relationships with people even though on occasion people will disappoint, aggravate and, in some cases, make my blood boil. I am certain that there are people I would have never encountered had it not been for God's leading me into entrepreneurship. Everyone that has come into my life, no matter if only briefly, seasonally, or still present today, has purpose within my assignment. Here is the spiritual component…I, too, have purpose in their divine assignment. Think about that for a moment.

Do any of the above co-pilot tendencies resonate with you? Maybe you have a few co-pilot tendencies that are not shown above. Here is what's so amazing: God knew each of us before we were born and He has been fully aware of our shortcomings from the beginning. My business, and quite frankly, every area of my life, has operated with greater ease with God as my pilot. I certainly do not want to mislead you into thinking that I don't encounter disappointments or hardships. In fact, those consultants who once followed my example and became Mary Kay Independent Sales Directors all decided not to maintain their leadership role and later ended their business. What I hope that you gain insight on through my experience is that what you believe to be your best day as an entrepreneur, when you have obtained your highest achievement to date, when you've received your highest paycheck to date, or even when you believe you have lived your best life to date, Ephesians 3:20 states, "Now to him who is able to do immeasurably more than all we ask or imagine, according to his power that is at work within us." *New International Version.* In other words, you have not seen the half of what God has in store for you. Be encouraged, entrepreneurs. There is amazing grace and an undeniable peace when God is your pilot.

"If God is your co-pilot, switch seats."

~ Unknown

Successful
D VA
Dynamic Independent Victorious Achiever

Pit 8 ~ Spending Profits Rather Than Saving & Investing

Over the course my corporate career, I spent a lot of time consulting with business owners on how to operate successful, profitable businesses. As an entrepreneur, I began to use some of the same strategies to successfully operate my own business. In my business, earning income comes as quick as selling a product. The more I sell, the more I earn. The profit margin on the products in my business is 50%. In simple terms, when a customer buys a product for $30, my profit is $15.

In the early stages of my business, while operating it on a part-time basis, my goal was to earn $300 - $400 profit per month. The driving force behind that goal was the monthly car payment on my Acura 3.2 TL, which was $342 per month. With a 50% profit from the sale of my products I became skilled at selling $650 - $700 in retail per month. In doing so, I had enough to pay the car payment and its insurance. As my skills and knowledge of the products improved, the amount of monthly income from my sales improved as well. For anyone desiring to own their own Mary Kay business, selling the products is the foundation of success. Thus, as a business owner who decided to lead others in operating their own Mary Kay business, it was my responsibility to coach others on how to earn their own desired level of income. As a result, even if they decided against becoming an Independent Sales Director, they could still earn great residual income simply from selling the products.

A profit earned is only as good as how it is used. One may define profit as the excess of returns over expenditures in one transaction or a series of transactions. Often times when business owners launch a business they believe that they are entitled to their business profits immediately. The reality is in some cases profits are not visible for several years after the launch of a business. Bad money management could sink your business faster than anything else. On my own journey as an entrepreneur, I have experienced loss. I have experienced the traditional loss, which occurs during the early years of business when personal or borrowed funds are used to launch a business. I have also experienced loss that resulted from simply not having a plan for income and expenses. What am I saying? I have not always utilized my profits wisely, and when operating a business based upon commissions, managing profits is of the utmost importance.

Money management is a topic that in my experience people tend to avoid. We all want to know how to earn business profits, and a lot of it, when in fact earning business profits is only the beginning. Managing your earned business profits is one of the main components to sustaining a healthy business and a desired personal lifestyle. One tool that assists me as an entrepreneur is a budget. I have lived off and on a budget throughout my entire adult life as well as during my years as an entrepreneur. Although a budget may appear to place constraints around what you want, that is really not the case at all. I have been the most financially sound in my personal finances as well as my business when operating with a budget. A budget is designed to provide future benefits based upon the creation of a spending plan. Budgets, similar to investments, are instruments that assist in managing the direction of your finances in the future. One of my primary responsibilities during my corporate career was to help business owners prepare and sustain a budget for their business. Why do you or I, as entrepreneurs, need a budget? A budget when followed and managed properly prevents you and me from spending (too much) time in **Pit 8.....Spending Profits Rather Than Saving & Investing.**

A budget is an estimate of income and expenses. It exposes spending habits no matter if they are good or bad. However, a budget places you and me in the position to direct where the money should go rather than wondering where the money went. A budget should display anticipated income to be earned and the expenses applicable for the operation of the business. Actual income and expenses are recorded and then compared against the budgeted amounts. Any differences should be analyzed and a budget must change when circumstances in the business change. Below is an example of a business budget.

MONTHLY BUDGET			
	Date _____		
INCOME	Budget/ Projection	Actual	Difference
OPERATING INCOME	$ 23,500	$ 23,000	$ (500)
OTHER	$ 2,500	$ 2,500	$ -
			$ -
TOTAL OPERATING INCOME	$ 26,000	$ 25,500	$ (500)
Interest Income_____	$ 500	$ 450	$ (50)
Other	$ -	$ -	$ -
TOTAL NON-OPERATING INCOME	$ 500	$ 450	$ (50)
TOTAL INCOME	$ 26,500	$ 25,950	$ (550)
EXPENSES			
Operating Expenses	$ 1,200	$ 1,100	$ 100
Accounting & Legal	$ 100	$ 350	$ (250)
Advertising	$ 100	$ -	$ 100
Depreciation	$ -	$ -	$ -
Dues & Subscriptions	$ 150	$ 150	$ -
Insurance	$ 4,000	$ 4,000	$ -
Internet	$ 125	$ 125	$ -
Maintenance	$ 1,500	$ 750	$ 750
Postage	$ 100	$ 100	$ -
Rent	$ 5,000	$ 5,000	$ -
Salaries & Wages	$ 6,000	$ 5,500	$ 500
Telephone	$ 250	$ 225	$ 25
Travel	$ -	$ -	$ -
Utilities	$ 450	$ 575	$ (125)
Other	$ -	$ -	$ -
TOTAL	$ 18,975	$ 17,875	$ 1,100
DEBTS			
Loan(s)	$ -	$ -	$ -
TOTAL	$ -	$ -	$ -
OTHER EXPENSES			
Other_____	$ -	$ -	$ -
Other_____	$ -	$ -	$ -
Other_____	$ -	$ -	$ -
TOTAL	$ -	$ -	$ -
TOTAL EXPENSES	$ 18,975	$ 17,875	$ 1,100
MONTHLY SURPLUS OR (SHORTAGE)	$ 7,525	$ 8,075	$ 550

As you can see from the above sample budget, the company budgeted for income of $26,500 with expenses of $18,975, thus creating a budgeted surplus of $7,525. When the actual income and expenses were compared against the budget, the company closed the month with a surplus of $8,075. You will notice that although the actual income was not as expected, the company saved on expenses. A business operating with a surplus has many advantages. The owner is in a position to have more liquid assets and there is a greater opportunity to save money in reserve for a time when the business' income may be lower. A budget is also an essential tool in the overall business plan when seeking funding from a financial institution.

I wish I could say that I have never experienced Pit #8. There were times, especially in the early years of business, when I could tell simply from the balance in my bank account that more money was going out than coming in. Earning income in my business arrives as quickly as selling a product. I had enough experience to know that I needed to create a budget, and I did. Why? Simply because no matter the amount of achievements or amount of success, none of it mattered unless I managed the income that was generated by my business. Thus, after recording all of my estimated income and expenses on paper, I discovered that for months I had operated in the red, or in other words, in the negative. My business expenses exceeded the amount of income. I certainly had no intention of operating my business for an extended period of time using personal or borrowed funds. Thus, I chose to modify and delete expenses where necessary while I worked my business to increase income. My education and experience in budgeting has taught me that budgets are only as good as the data being used to create them. Overstating income or using inaccurate expenses can cause a budget to be unrealistic.

Creating my budget, for both personal financial management and business management, compelled me to reduce and even eliminate unnecessary expenses. I became more aware of what expenses were absolutely necessary to operate efficiently. If your desire is to not be held in bondage by debt, or have a business that generates a healthy profit on a regular basis, you must be intentional about saving and investing. After all, one thing that is certain is that as entrepreneur in business, a rainy day will come and I am not talking about the weather.

"Do not save what is left after spending. Spend what is left after saving."

~ Warren Buffet

Pit 9 ~ Quitting

There is a saying that goes like this: "Quitters never win and winners never quit." Well, some winners do quit. Winners resign or take a step away from the arenas in which they were once successful and known for their achievements. I am a sports fan and a few of the people that I grew up watching win week after week were Joe Montana (San Francisco 49ers), Michael Jordan (Chicago Bulls) and Jerry Rice (San Francisco 49ers). It is no secret that each of these athletes enjoyed successful careers. However, a time arrived in their careers when it was best to step away from their calling as professional athletes. They each quit on favorable terms after enormous amounts of success, and more importantly, after establishing a legacy for others to follow. I would say that they quit "on top of their game."

I am going to go out on a limb and say most entrepreneurs have had some experience, arrived at some moment, or even went through a season where the brief thought of quitting arose. Although there are times and valid reasons why people must close their business or make the decision to quit, when one is about to fall into **Pit 9.....Quitting,** this is the time be sure that you are not quitting for trivial reasons. In other words, don't quit at the bottom of your game, when the chips are down, or for failing to accept responsibility for the success of your business. A few questions to ask yourself when thoughts of quitting arise:

1. Am I quitting because of burn out?

2. Am I doing too much or too little?

3. Am I taking on something that God has not assigned to me?

4. Am I working the business out of obligation (this means you "know how" to operate the business, but you lack passion for the business)?

Considering giving up is not new. The Bible has several examples of those who wanted to quit. One of the most notable examples is when Peter and the disciples had been fishing all night with no results for their efforts. Ready to quit, Peter lowered his nets on the ground of Jesus' word and they caught so much fish that their nets began to break. Giving up is never an easy decision. Yet, there is something to be said about being obedient to God's word and the vision He has placed in the heart of an entrepreneur. You may not understand God's directives and why He wants it done a certain way, but His way is always for your good. There is success in obedience.

Nonetheless, there have been times when I meandered into quit pit. There were several trivial reasons that caused my quit pit experience. However, none of them were compelling enough to cause me to follow through with quitting. In other words, I did not remain in Pit 9 and allow its darkness to compel me to quit. These reasons may or may not be relevant to your business, but they have all caused me, at one point or another, to question why should I keep going in my business.

1. Disappointment in others who say one thing and do another.

2. Cancelled appointments. In my business, I rely on the word of others to keep their appointments. A cancelled appointment for what seems to be an invalid reason is frustrating. When too many cancelled appointments occur in one week, or over a short period of time, it gets annoying.

3. Income inconsistency.

4. Unable to reach a goal that I have been pursuing for years.

I believe clearly that as Peter and the disciples were given instructions to not quit and were redirected in an effort to fulfill God's will for their lives, I, too, have been steered into a direction to fulfill God's will for my life. Quitting can either be the plan or it could interrupt God's plan. I am grateful that I am in communication with God so that during times when I have had longer than normal pity parties, I can discern when it is best to pivot, reassess, readjust, or simply reset my compass. Missing a goal, in my opinion, is not a sufficient reason to quit. I have missed quite a few and frankly the disappointment was a weight on my shoulders. Over the course of my 13 years as an entrepreneur I have seen many Independent Beauty Consultants and Independent Sales Directors, some of whom accepted my teaching, coaching and mentorship and rose to the top 2% of the independent sales force in their Mary Kay businesses, choose to quit their business for one reason or another. I have learned that as an entrepreneur, who has been called to lead others in business, to do whatever it takes to avoid the mental anguish that can come when others that I have helped choose to quit. One of the things that helped me overcome and come out of the quit pit is faith. Faith has unbelievable power when used. A second helping hand out of the quit pit is perseverance. The decision to persevere has allowed me the opportunity to exercise my "going through" muscles. The enemy wanted me to quit. Yet, I decided to press through in an effort to be able to help someone else out of her/his quit pit. I truly believe that there are people that God has aligned for me to encounter, encourage, inspire and empower. Being able to go through periods of earning inconsistent income has allowed me to be more cognizant of personal spending and budgeting. Bouncing back from the disappointment of cancelled appointments gives me the ability to be more forgiving and understanding. Overcoming the disappointments of seeing others quit provided an opportunity for me to learn how to keep moving forward as an effective business leader to others while not taking personal their decision and action to quit. It all provides a testimony and experience that can be shared with others.

In 2011, after being in business for 6 years, I believed that I was being positioned to reach the highest achievement that a Mary Kay Independent Sales Director could achieve - a Mary Kay Independent National Sales Director. Independent National Sales Directors hold the most prestigious position among Independent Sales Directors. The position of Independent National Sales Director provides a platform of massive influence and I was (and still am) looking forward to being an example for others to pursue this level of achievement in their business. Of all the trivial reasons shown above that have caused me to flirt with the danger of the quit pit, the one that gives me the most frustration is being unable to reach the goal of becoming a Mary Kay Independent National Sales Director. It does not help when others who have seen, been a part of, or contributed to the success of my business make comments such as, "Andrea should have been a Mary Kay Independent National Sales Director long ago." I have always, in some way, held a level of leadership responsibility during all of my corporate career and entrepreneurial experience. I am certain that the ability to lead others is one of my many gifts from God. I am also certain that I have been called to empower and be an example for others. However, God's timing, my timing and the timing of others for me to receive this promotion are not in synch. Thank God for his perfect time and plan for my life.

Although achievement and goal attainment bring me joy, I am not a woman whose identity is tied to the spotlight or being in positions of influence and power. Anyone who genuinely knows me knows that I am humble and focused. The platform of Independent National Sales Director has always been viewed in my sight as a conduit to do what I am called to do for God's glory. But when seeking to achieve the next biggest goal, I neglected to value the main purpose, which is to please God. Through my relationship with God, I have been able to see that I was obviously not ready for the amount of responsibility that being an Independent National Sales Director would bring. While experiencing the achievements that include earning the use of 5 Mary Kay Career Cars by 2011, building a base of over 200 customers whom I serviced with skin care and cosmetics products and leading 9 women to the esteemed position of Independent Sales Director, it was still not my time. What does helping to develop 9 offspring Sales Directors mean in terms of numbers? Developing 9 offspring Sales Directors means that I have had an impact in the lives of over 270 entrepreneurs. The 9 offspring Sales Directors does not include the number of people who elect not to pursue leadership positions within their business. In spite of that, it was not my time.

The development of offspring Sales Directors is the driving force behind becoming a Mary Kay Independent National Sales Director. The end result to be considered for the position of Independent National Sales Director is to develop a total of 20 Independent Sales Directors. I was practically one-half of the way there, but God said "no." All 9 offspring Sales Directors, over the span of 4 years (2011 – 2015), relinquished their leadership position in business. To date, some of them are still in my area as Consultants and some have totally quit the business. So, what happened one may ask? I used to ask God that question quite often. Thank God for his unselfish love that allows me the time to develop my ability to emotionally handle loss, setbacks and delay. When God gives favor and decides to promote me to this esteemed platform, He will sustain me. His light will shine bright and compel others to get involved and it will be the women divinely called to be a part of my National Area.

"The moment you want to quit is usually the moment right before something amazing happens."

~ Unknown

Pit 10 ~ Surrender....The Pit to Palace Experience

Faith and perseverance, added with a dose of obedience, is what prevented me from quitting. I have come to the place as a business owner to know that God's favor and divine timing bring about the best promotions. Yet, I had not given my full attention to the one thing that God wanted from me in my business.

At the beginning of 2017, as I entered my 12th year in business, I recall one day sitting and having one of my many conversations with God. He and I were discussing some of the results that came about in my business from forcing things to happen and trying to keep open or knock down doors that God had closed for my good. I was sick and tired of setting big goals and missing them. I was exhausted from putting together training topics to assist the Independent Beauty Consultants in reaching the goals they "said" they wanted to achieve, but failed to back up what with action. There was no use for a pity party because the speed of the leader is the speed of the gang – right? Well, to make profound changes in my life I decided to be the change I wanted to see. I wanted and needed something different. My achievements to date had been wonderful, but I knew God had more in store for me. The vision and dream of being an Independent National Sales Director is still to this day alive. That particular day during the conversation with God I acknowledged that I had to release some things, lose some things, change some behaviors, dismiss some people, forgive some people, forgive myself and ultimately, SURRENDER to God's will.

Surrender can be an intimidating word. The word itself seems to go against our very innate desire for independence. If you have ever had to surrender against your will, then there could be several uncomfortable emotions that rise up when you ponder the word. However, surrender was what I was clearly being instructed to do. The reality is I had tried operating my business as the pilot with God as the co-pilot. In spite of all that I had experienced over the prior 12 years I still had not lived my best life as an entrepreneur. The greatest act that seemed binding and limiting, while simultaneously would free me, was to completely place every decision, every plan and every outcome into the capable hands of God. God disclosed to me that without a complete and intentional surrender to the former, I would never experience the magnitude of what was destined for my life and business. It was time to do something different. Following my acceptance and commitment to completely surrender my business to God, I was led to the book of Genesis and the story of Joseph.

As I began to read and study the story of Joseph in the book of Genesis the first thing I did was outline his heritage on paper. I tracked his lineage and studied the dynamics of his family. Every good and bad thing that occurred in Joseph's life and the lives of his family was intentional. Even the names of his children, Manasseh and Ephraim, who arrived later in his life, bring reference back to his childhood and into his future. In short, Joseph was born in the lineage of Abraham. Abraham, at 100 years of age, and Sarah had a son named Isaac. Isaac married Rebekah, who had twin sons, Esau and Jacob. Jacob wed two wives, Leah and Rachel, who were sisters and, in actuality, his cousins. Among Leah, Rachel and their two handmaids, Jacob was the father of 12 sons and 1 daughter. It was Rachel who gave birth to Joseph. Joseph, at the tender age of 17, began to share his dreams. His brothers were extremely jealous of Joseph because they perceived that their father loved Joseph more than them. Joseph's dreams revealed that he indeed would, one day, reign as their ruler. Naturally, his brothers despised him even more and plotted to get rid of him.

Joseph, after being stripped of his beautiful coat that was a gift from his father, ended up being thrown into a pit. Isn't it amazing how people believed to have our best interest at heart think that putting us down will actually lift them up? As the story continues, Joseph ended up being sold by his brothers, for 20 pieces of silver, to the Ishmaelites, who in turn sold Joseph to Potiphar, an officer of Pharaoh, in Egypt. Joseph's time in Egypt was critical to the destiny of his life because he still had the gift of interpreting dreams. Although made to be a slave, God was with Joseph. As I studied Joseph's life and how he handled his time in prison, I began to see how Joseph's life modeled what it means to surrender to God's will. He could have endured his days in prison holding a grudge against his brothers, the prison warden and even Pharaoh himself. Joseph received God's favor in the sight of the prison warden - and ultimately with Pharaoh - by being able to use his gift. He made lemonade out of lemons. He interpreted the dreams of those who were confined with him. Pharaoh eventually requested that Joseph be brought to him to interpret his dreams. One of the key verses of this encounter with Pharaoh shows how Joseph honored God for his ability to interpret dreams: "Joseph answered Pharaoh, It is not in me; God [not I] will give Pharaoh a [favorable] answer of peace." *Genesis 41:16 - New International Version.* This verse reminded me of my time operating my business as the pilot. I did give thanks to God; however, I never acknowledged that it was by God's power that I was able to do what I was doing. Joseph continued to interpret the dreams of Pharaoh. The dreams did come true as interpreted and Joseph was placed in charge of Pharaoh's house. All the people therein would obey Joseph and his command; only matters of the throne would still be handled by Pharaoh. The story chronicles the first 30 years of Joseph's life, during which he, for all intents and purposes, surrendered and was elevated by God from the **Pit to the Palace**.

Joseph's story has given me renewed hope and an unwavering commitment to what surrender really means. The pit of surrender has been a must needed pit stop for me. Above and beyond any other pit that either I found myself in or managed to avoid, it is this pit that has meant the most to me. I dare to believe that we all must spend some time in this pit in order to experience the fullness of God's plan for our lives. I can attest that I have learned a few lessons and discovered more about myself while in this pit. Here are few of these discoveries:

1. I have learned what I can live without ~ Philippians 4:11

2. I have learned who I cannot live without ~ Philippians 4:11

3. My level of faith has dramatically elevated ~ Hebrews 11:1

4. My prayer life is constant ~ Philippians 4:6

5. I am more confident ~ Hebrews 10:35 - 37

6. I have been able to discern and hear God's voice more clearly for direction ~ Psalm 32:8

7. I am more obedient ~ 1 Samuel 15:22

8. I am less emotionally attached when disappointment occurs ~ John 14:27

9. I am quicker to make changes in my business when directed by Him ~ Psalm 62:5

10. I am thankful for everything because I believe in God's will for my life and business ~ 1 Thessalonians 5:18

As the story continues, you will discover that Joseph's dreams did come true. God's favor did place him in position of influence. Essentially, Joseph became a highly respected leader, placed in charge of a land and its people that would go through famine and abundance. I encourage you to read the entire 50 chapters of Genesis. You will discover and learn to appreciate the story of a young man whose life was divinely orchestrated by God. I believe I was led to study Joseph's story for several reasons. As an entrepreneur, I hold a position of influence over others who rely upon my leadership to help them be successful entrepreneurs, in which they (and I) could go through periods of famine and abundance. In spite of being thrown in a pit and sold, Joseph operated from a posture of surrender. His dreams were the mouthpiece of truth and he always shared the truth about himself and others exactly how God revealed it to him.

From the place of surrender I have truly discovered my life's purpose, which is to live every day intentionally being the best I can be and inspiring others to do the same. God wants each of us to live our lives on purpose fulfilling His will. One of the best ways to hear from God and know His will is to be still and surrender. Surrender brings peace. Surrender allows us to view and experience everything God has promised in His word for our lives. Surrender provides an ease in which to do as God asks us to do in 1 Peter 5:7. "Cast all your anxiety on him because he cares for you." *New International Version*

If you have had an experience such as Joseph and are still waiting for God to elevate you to your palace, allow Joseph's and the pit lessons in this book to encourage you. In my humble opinion, pits are oftentimes placed in our lives for God to get our attention. I don't know what my palatial location or ultimate elevated position in business will look like, but I do believe that as was the case with Joseph, I too am going to remain in a posture of surrender. While I continue to experience and live the entrepreneurial life, I intend to seek God's guidance for my business. I desire to operate in His will for my life. Be encouraged and hang on in there. I AM!

"Joseph did not endure the pit, Potiphar's house and prison because he knew he would end up in Pharaoh's palace. He simply remained faithful wherever he found himself. God did the rest."

~ H. B Charles Jr.

About the Author

Andrea Evans-Dixon is a native Floridian born and raised in Clearwater, Florida. She earned her Bachelor of Science Degree in Financial Business Management from Florida Southern College. Her hobbies are reading, shopping and cruising. However, her most cherished leisure activity is spending quiet time in conversation and hearing from God.

She is passionate about helping people live their best lives and in particular seeing others rise to platforms of leadership. She believes that everyone has light that must shine to fully fulfill God's plan and purpose in their lives. From whatever platform that God deems suitable to use her she will continue to lift others up, share ideas and seek to inspire others to greatness. In the words from a poem penned by Mary Kay Ash,

> "On Silver Wings"
> I have a premonition
> That soars on silver wings.
> It's a dream of your accomplishment
> Of many wondrous things.
>
> I do not know beneath which sky
> Or where you'll change fate.
> I only know it will be high!
> I only know it will be **great!**

www.ingramcontent.com/pod-product-compliance
Lightning Source LLC
Chambersburg PA
CBHW032017190326
41520CB00007B/506